His
Amish
Baby
BOOK ONE

Katie King

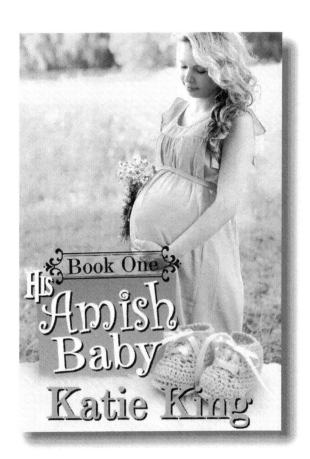

His Amish Baby: Book One

Copyright © 2016 by Katie King

This novel is a work of fiction, and is the sole work of the author's imagination. Events and places bear no witness to true events or persons, past or present. Names, Characters, and events are used fictitiously. Any likeness to actual persons, past or present, living or dead, are purely coincidental, and beyond the intent of the author.

All scripture references by Zondervan NIV

All rights reserved. No part of this book may be reproduced in any form either written or electronically without written permission from the author.

Glossary of Terms:
ach—oh
boppli, bopplin—baby, babies
brudder—brother
danki—thank you
dat—dad
dawdi haus—guest house, cottage for grandparents
dochder—daughter
Englisch, Englischer—non-Amish
*family*e—family
fraa—wife
Gott—God
grossdaddi--grandfather
grossmammi—grandmother
gudemariye—good morning
gut—good
haus—house
hochzich—wedding
jah—yes
kaffi—coffee
kapp—Amish head covering
kinner—children
kumme—come in

mamm—mom
mann—husband, man
mei—me, my
mudder—mother
naerfich—nervous
narrish—foolish, crazy
nee—no
rumschpringe—run around time for Amish youth before they take the baptism
schweschder—sister
shemt—ashamed
vadder—father
wie gehts—how are you
wilkume—welcome

> Trust in the Lord with all thine heart; and lean not unto thine own understanding. in all thy ways acknowledge Him, and He shall direct thy paths.
>
> Proverbs 3: 5-6

Trust in the Lord with all your heart, and lean not unto your own understanding. Proverbs 3:5

Chapter One

Noah Byler tilted his head slightly, enjoying the warmth of the August sun on his face as he tied his horse to the post of the parking meter downtown. Digging into the pocket of his broadfall pants, he found a couple of dimes and slid them into the slot of the meter.

There was the slightest hint of autumn in the air as he looked up at the swaying leaves on the trees overhead. He stared at them for a moment, already mourning their loss, as it represented the passing of a year that had gone by too quickly.

This would be his last trip to town for such an occasion, as he'd prayed long and with much devotion over the trip that had become a crutch to him. He knew he couldn't keep hoping she'd come back to him this way, and hanging out in town waiting for his betrothed the way he had for the past year was not doing anything but keeping him from moving on with his life.

He shook off the uneasy feeling he had, and walked up the path to the park, determined to enjoy his weekly ritual for the last time.

It was Monday afternoon, his one day every week when his sister, Belinda, was too preoccupied with her laundry chore to notice if he slipped away for a couple of hours just to breathe. Truth be told, he'd walked an imaginary line on which he'd teetered, ever since Simon and Miranda had gone away for their *rumschpringe*—without him.

Monday afternoons were his only respite from the heavy burden of responsibility that was his reality.

He and Simon had begun planning for their respite from the community well before he and Miranda had begun courting. Soon after, she'd been eager to join them for their once-in-a-lifetime adventure.

They'd all planned to leave that sunny, Monday afternoon nearly a year ago, just like they had every year before that, until Simon finally made up his mind to go without his best friend. Time had almost run out for them, as their parents had nagged them to join the church, and so they left to avoid missing out on the final days of their *rumschpringe*.

Noah had already talked himself out of going before he'd even gotten there. The corn was in need of harvesting, and firewood needed to be split for the winter. Too many chores awaited him at home. Chores his sister could not do without his help.

They'd held back too many years, waiting for Noah to have the guts to leave his sister behind and live his life, but he couldn't let go of his responsibility to her, no matter what was at stake. She hadn't a husband, and had given up her chance after the death of their parents, and she'd made the sacrifice for him. Seth had been courting her at the time, and decided he didn't want to take responsibility for young Noah alongside her. In the end, he ran off and married Priscilla, Belinda's best friend.

It had almost broken her.

She mourned the loss for a long time, and it had made her bitter. Noah thought she would have been better off if he'd been old enough to take care of himself at that time so she could have had her life apart from the responsibility of taking care of him. Because of this, once he became old enough, he hadn't the heart or the conscience to leave her behind.

Lately, he often found himself wondering if they'd have both been better off if she'd married and had a life of her own. He'd wanted to marry Miranda, and had felt selfish wanting such a thing when his own sister had given up her chance for his sake.

In the end, he'd let Miranda go without him.

He didn't feel he had the luxury of taking his *rumschpringe*, even though it was his right of passage as an Amish youth. But Belinda had been left with the responsibility of taking care of him when she was only seventeen years old, and had given up her time of freedom to take care of him.

It sometimes angered him that he'd lost his best friend, and the girl he'd intended on marrying because of his debt to his sister, until he reminded himself of the sacrifices she'd made for him.

Nearly one year before, he'd left Simon and Miranda here at this very spot, and he'd regretted it every day since. Because of this, every Monday after that day, he returned hoping for some sort of closure.

Today was no different.

His heart ached for Miranda, but it was time to let her go. He was in need of some wise words from his best friend, whom he'd known since birth, but even he was gone. He and Simon had always lived next door to one another, and when Noah's parents had died just after his thirteenth birthday, Simon had been there for him while he mourned deeply.

He'd helped Noah finish the planting that year, and had even stayed by his side while he'd brought in the harvest so that he and his sister wouldn't go without food over the long winter months. For ten more years after his parent's death, he and Simon worked side-by-side, becoming men before their time. Now, he felt as if he'd lived an entire lifetime, even though he hadn't done much living at all.

Noah wasn't sure which of them he missed more, but he missed Simon and Miranda differently for obvious reasons. All he knew was that his life had not been the same since they'd left the community.

Sinking down on the edge of the fountain in the center of the park, he listened to the pigeons cooing, as they fought for leftover bits of food discarded by the people who worked downtown, and usually ate at the fountain during their lunch hour.

Across the street, a couple arguing shifted his attention from his own woes.

The young, *Englisch* pair didn't seem to mind that their voices carried along the breeze and reverberated between the buildings, exaggerating the emotions that seemed to flair into a higher pitch with every accusation of the quarrelsome duet.

They had a familiarity that disturbed Noah, the young woman's gestures taking him back to a time when he was certain he'd witnessed them before.

Her blond hair that rested on her shoulders flipped around in the breeze, the hem of her short pink dress fluttering around her knees. Her shoulders shuddered with sobs, while her hand continuously flew up to cover her mouth as though she was terrified of the words being spoken to her. From this distance, she reminded him of Miranda, but he'd seen her in a lot of women over the last year, and in the end, they had always turned out to be someone else.

Like all the others, this young woman was *Englisch*, and the young man with her was *Englisch*. He seemed shifty to Noah, his baseball cap covering his face, but he could see the anger in his gestures, and the volume in which he shouted at the poor girl. His unstable gait suggested he'd been drinking heavily, but the young woman seemed determined to stay in the heated conversation.

Feeling unrest by the situation, Noah decided to keep an eye on them. He wasn't altogether certain why, as he'd always minded his own business, especially when the *Englisch* were involved. This time, he made up his mind to get a closer look.

For some reason, he felt prompted to see if he could somehow stop the argument. He supposed he feared for the young woman's safety when the man lurched toward her, his arms flailing.

At the crosswalk on the opposite side of the street, his dread increased when he recognized the man's voice. He would know his friend's voice anywhere. Though the two of them were shouting over the traffic, he was unable to hear the words, but he feared it was Simon.

As he waited impatiently for the light to change so he could cross, blood rushed to his head when he realized the woman was Miranda.

Even though her back was to him the entire time, he recognized her voice. She was arguing out on the street with Simon. Noah waved to him, hoping to divert his attention, but he was too preoccupied putting his finger in her face. What could cause them to argue, or for Simon to treat her with such disrespect?

Noah stood at the corner, anxiously waiting for the traffic to clear when Simon hauled back and struck Miranda in the face with the back of his hand. He darted out in front of a car, the car horn blasting, but Noah had only Miranda's safety on his mind. He weaved through another lane of traffic, but before he could, Simon struck her again.

"Stop it!" he shouted over the traffic, but neither of them heard him.

Feeling the urgency to reach her, his own safety was not an issue when he walked out in front of a car, causing it to slam on its breaks and stop just inches from his moving frame. The commotion caused Miranda to turn around fully.

His eyes fixed on her swelled abdomen as he stopped in the middle of the road, staring at the woman he loved.

His Miranda was pregnant, and it was obvious Simon was the father.

Chapter Two

Noah

She'd barely uttered the word above a whisper, but he could see, even from the middle of the road, that was the word her lips had formed.

He stood frozen in the middle of the road, staring with unbelieving eyes, even though she was right in front of him.

His gaze darted to Simon, who, by this time, had spotted him standing there. He, too, stood motionless, but only for a moment. Noah waited for the traffic to clear, feeling anxious to get across to her, though every instinct in him screamed at him to turn around and walk away.

With her back to Simon, he grabbed Miranda by her arm and forced her around to look at him. "What is he doing here? Are you here to meet up with him?"

"I don't know," she sobbed. "I swear; I wasn't here to meet him."

Simon reached down and grabbed the suitcase at her feet and flipped it open, allowing her things to spill out onto the sidewalk. She buried her face in her hands and sobbed, while Simon continued to accuse her of betraying him.

Noah watched in disbelief, feeling helplessly unable to cross the street because of rush-hour traffic flowing through the busy main street downtown.

Deciding he could wait no longer, he held up a hand to stop traffic, and then began to step into the road. Amazingly, the cars stopped, and he was able to get across both lanes, but not before

Miranda collapsed to the ground in the pile of her things that were strewn all over the sidewalk.

He approached Simon. "What's going on here?"

"This is none of your business, goody-two-shoes," Simon said, slurring his words. "Go back home to the community where you belong, and leave us to our problems. This doesn't concern you."

He could smell the alcohol on Simon's breath, even at the distance he stood from him.

"This does concern me," Noah said with a raised voice. "You've obviously been drinking, and you're not thinking clearly. I'm not going to stand around and watch you hit her! She's pregnant; what's the matter with you?"

"Go home, Noah," Simon barked at him. "I told you, this is not your business. This is between me and Miranda."

Noah looked down at Miranda scrambling to pick up her things. "The two of you are my friends, and that makes it my business."

He cringed at the word "friends", knowing he had once wanted to marry Miranda.

"Well, by the look of her," Simon accused. "maybe the two of you have been more than friends!"

"What are you talking about Simon? I haven't seen either of you in almost a year; not since that day I dropped you off here, remember?"

"Why is it that I see both of you here today, and she has a suitcase packed? I had no idea she was pregnant, and when I found her here, she accused me of being the father. It's clear to me that *you're* the father, and she's nothing but a liar!"

"I'm not a liar. I'm going back home," Miranda said, still sitting on the ground, picking up her things and stuffing them back into her suitcase. "I wasn't meeting him here. I was going to take the bus."

Noah crouched down on his haunches and began to help her, but then his gaze met hers. Her red-rimmed eyes and bruised cheek saddened him.

God help him, he still loved her.

"*Ach,* I know I'm not the *vadder* of your *boppli,*" he said gently. "Is Simon really the *vadder*?"

Her lower lip quivered and her eyes filled with fresh tears. "Yes," she said quietly. "He is the father of my baby, but he doesn't believe me."

Noah helped her up from the ground, and then sneered at Simon. "That's his sorry luck if he doesn't believe it."

Simon grabbed for her arm, but Noah shoved him away. "Don't put your hands on her again, I'm warning you!"

"You don't scare me, Noah; you never did." he said, swiping at him.

He missed, but Noah clipped his jaw with a right hook, and then Simon hit him back.

Noah stepped back, determined to end the fight before things went any further. "I'll take you home, Miranda."

Simon turned to her. "So you're leaving with Noah, and that's it? That isn't doing anything to convince me he isn't the father of that baby."

"I'm going home, and I pray that my family won't shun me," she said, still sobbing.

Noah would gladly take her home, but he already knew her stern father would turn her away. She looked just as *Englisch* as she sounded. Had a mere year changed the both of them so much that their entire upbringing had left them?

Sirens that had been off in the distance, suddenly grew louder. Noah talked over the noise. "I'm going to ask you this only once, Simon. Are you the *vadder* of her *boppli*?"

"I couldn't be, it's impossible."

"Were you living together?"

"We stayed together for the first two months, until I realized what a mistake that was. All she did was nag me to stop drinking and having fun!"

"That sounds like some *gut* advice," Noah said, blowing out a heavy sigh. "Since she stayed with you, is it possible that you're the *vadder*?"

"No! It isn't possible; she's a liar."

Two police cars rounded the corner on Main Street and parked in front of the diner where the three of them stood. The officers got out of their vehicles and approach them, while a waitress in the diner came running out to greet the officers.

"That's the one, Officers!" she said, pointing to Simon. "He's the one who hit that pregnant girl. Arrest him!"

Chapter Three

Officers aggressively surrounded Simon, one of them taking hold of his arm. "Did you hit that young lady?" They asked him.

"Take your hands off me! I didn't hit her; we were arguing that's all. And it's nobody's business but ours."

Noah couldn't believe how his friend was acting. Had he always been like this, or had being away from the community changed him that much, or was it the alcohol that altered his good judgment?

"It's our business if you hit her," the officer said. "I'm going to ask you again; did you hit her?"

Simon looked at the officer. "And I'm telling you again," he said, swaggering a little. "I didn't hit her. You can even ask her yourself."

Noah helped Miranda to her feet as he put the last of her things back in the suitcase.

"Did this man hit you?" the officer asked her.

She shook her head. "We were arguing; that's all."

Her eyes cast downward, and she grabbed the handle of her suitcase. "I have to go home," she said nervously.

Noah placed a gentle hand on Miranda's arm, and she reluctantly looked at him. "Why are you defending him? I saw him hit you! Granted, I was in the middle of the street, but I saw the whole thing."

"I saw it too," the waitress said, pointing to the diner behind them. "From the window right here. I'm the one who called 911."

The officer grabbed his handcuffs from his belt and began to place them on Simon. "You're under arrest for assault of a pregnant woman. Do you understand how serious this is? Assaulting a pregnant woman comes with a pretty hefty sentence, young man."

"Please don't take him to jail," Miranda begged. "I don't want my baby's father to be in jail."

"I'm going to have to ask you to step back, Miss, because we're going to arrest him. I have two eye-witnesses right here, and by the look of those bruises on your face, I can see neither of you are telling the truth. I don't know why you're protecting him, other than you don't want him to go to jail, but you've got to understand this is serious." the officer told her.

She felt dizzy, and the warm air had seemingly sucked the air from her lungs. She collapsed against Noah's sturdy frame, bright speckles of light flashing in her eyes.

When the other officer finished reading Simon his rights, they walked him over to the police car and put him in.

"Thanks for stabbing me in the back, Noah, after all the help I gave you. I guess you're the baby's father after all—and we're no longer friends!"

The words hurt Noah to the very core, but he clenched his jaw to stifle his emotions. He had Miranda to take care of, and she needed him to be strong. He held her close, trying to shelter her from the pain of it, but she'd heard every harsh word.

After giving her name to the officers, Noah offered his address to them to keep her family from knowing some of the trouble she was in. They both stood there and watched the police cars leaving with Simon in the back, and Miranda began to sob all over again, burying her face in his chest.

"Why did you lie to them?"

"Because I didn't want my baby's father to go to jail."

"This isn't your fault, Miranda," he said sternly. "He did this to himself—to all three of you!"

He supposed he understood her hesitance to get authorities involved, as it was the Amish way to handle things on their own, but this was out of their hands now.

The only thing he didn't understand, was the relationship between the two of them, and how it got to be the mess that it had gotten to be now. It was obvious to Noah that Simon had changed a great deal in the year since leaving the community, but so had Miranda. He was almost grateful that he hadn't left the community after seeing the changes that ruined two—no, three lives. Never mind how it was affecting him at the moment.

He took her suitcase from her, and took her hand in his. "Let's go. I'm taking you home."

Chapter Four

"I have a confession to make," Miranda said, breaking the awkward silence between them.

He assisted her into the buggy and then climbed in beside her. He was almost afraid to ask what it was that she wanted to confess so badly to him, but his curiosity got the better of him.

"My ears are all yours," he said to her, trying to make light of the situation.

"I did come here today because I knew you'd be here."

"The only way you would know that is if you had seen me the previous weeks." He wasn't sure how he felt about that, and busied himself backing the horse, and setting him on course toward Main Street.

"I admit I've been coming here every Monday since you dropped me off. I sit across the street at the diner and watch you. I've wished and hoped every week that I'd have enough courage to approach you or speak to you. Mostly, I came here wishing that I could take back the day you dropped me off. I wish things could go back to the way they were, but I know that isn't possible."

He looked down at her swelling belly, and felt guilty for wishing the same thing.

"Wishing a thing like that," he said sadly, "would be like wishing away your *boppli*, and I know you wouldn't do that. Not the Miranda I know."

She sobbed harder. "I wish I could take it back. I wish I could take it all back. I wish I would've married you instead of leaving."

He put his arm around her and pulled her close, shushing her and tilting his face to kiss her hair.

"I know you're upset now, but when you think about it, and think about your *boppli,* you'll realize that's not a good wish to make."

"Every Monday when I'd see you sitting out there at the fountain, you always looked so sad, and all I wanted to do was go to you and unburden my own sadness. But I couldn't go to you like this." She rolled her hand over her belly.

"Why were you here today?"

"I met Simon to tell him about the baby. I was going to give him a chance to let me come back and stay with him, but he rejected me and the baby. It didn't matter, because he still hadn't gotten a job, and he was rooming with two other guys, whose parents were paying their way, and he was so drunk, I wish I would have kept my mouth shut. I had nowhere else to go, and I thought he'd changed, but he's worse than he was when I left the apartment we'd shared. At that time, he was almost out of money, and I thought if I left, he'd be forced to get a job, but he found someone else to mooch off instead of me. I'd been working at the bakery here in town, and I was supporting both of us. I got upset the day before I left when he'd spent our rent money on beer; I had just found out I was pregnant, and I didn't want him around the baby. I had to take a pay-cut to live in the loft above the bakery. But I'm so close to delivering that I had to leave the job because I had to be on my feet so many hours. I realize I can't take care of a baby on my own and I need my family. I only hope they won't shun me when they see that I'm pregnant and don't have a husband. I knew that if something went wrong, and Simon was as I expected him to be, that perhaps you would be kind enough to give me a ride home since I have very little money left."

"What about Simon?" He asked cringing at the question. "Do you think the two of you will marry?"

"He said he doesn't want to marry me. He said the baby was a mistake, and he doesn't want anything to do with either of us. After he hit me today, and seeing him so drunk, I don't want anything to do with him. Not ever!"

"If he was rejecting you and the *boppli,* then why was he fussing about it so much and accusing me of being the *vadder*?"

She shrugged. "I suppose that's his way of getting rid of his own guilt. I believe he wants me to take the responsibility on my own, and if he can accuse you of being the father, I'm guessing he's hoping that you'll take responsibility for the both of us.

But I know it's not your responsibility, and I don't expect that from you. I know that your proposal of marriage to me expired when I left here without you. I want you to know how sorry I am that I did that. I've missed you every day since. I know it seems like I may have fallen in love with Simon, but honestly, I'm ashamed to say I was trying to fill the void of losing you. When you didn't go with us, I thought you were rejecting me, and it hurt me a great deal. I was lost without you, and Simon was there—in the beginning, anyway. I've been living on my own in the loft above the bakery ever since, and using nearly every penny I make just to pay my bills, and I can't do it anymore; especially now that I can't work. And with the baby coming, I can't work and pay a babysitter, and pay all the bills too. Simon refused to help me, and now I wouldn't take any help from him. He won't even get a job. He's living with guys that I don't approve of, and his drinking has become a bigger problem than I ever thought it could."

"I'm sorry for everything you had to go through, but I've been going through some things of my own. I've missed you terribly," he admitted. "We'll always be friends, no matter what. Let's get you home so you can get some rest because I know the stress is not good for the *boppli*."

She nodded, saying a silent prayer she would be welcomed by her family.

Chapter Five

Noah drove the buggy into the driveway he hadn't been in for almost a year. It was the driveway that led to Miranda's family home.

There used to be a time when nothing could keep him out of this driveway, or up on the porch sipping lemonade with her. But those days were gone.

Now it was foreign to both of them.

Things had changed. They were grown up, and she was pregnant. Things would never be the same again.

He stopped his horse and got out to grab her suitcase. Setting it on the ground, he helped her out of the buggy once again as if it was the most natural thing in the world. He pulled her hand into his in an effort to calm her, and led her up the stairs of the porch while she stared blankly.

He knocked on the door, and they waited—listening for footfalls over the pounding of their hearts. Both had reason to be nervous, and both had reason to doubt a positive outcome.

"I feel funny knocking on the door to my own house," she said. "But it's been too long since I've lived here, and I fear they won't be welcoming me or my baby."

She knew it was the dinner hour, and her dad would come to the door, ready to invite whoever was there to share their meal. She prayed he would have the same attitude toward his own daughter.

Her heart beat faster as she heard her father's footsteps nearing the door.

"I'm scared! I can't do this. Let's come back later after I've had time to think about what I'm going to say."

Noah squeezed her hand. "Don't be *naerfich*, I think the *boppli* says it all. Give them a minute for it to sink in, and let them speak first. But choose your answers carefully."

She sucked in a breath and held it there until the door swung open and her eyes met with her father's. She let the air out smoothly, slowly, as his gaze traveled first, to her short hair that hung loosely on her shoulders, and then to her obviously swollen belly. Then, he looked over at Noah, his expression full of anger and disappointment.

"Dad—*Dat,* I've come home,"

"Where is your *mann*?" he asked gruffly.

By this time, her mother had approached the door and pushed past her husband, pulling her daughter in her arms and sobbing. "*Ach,* I'm going to be a *grossmammi!*" she said in between sobs.

"Elma, go into the house this instant!"

She held fast to her daughter, defying her husband.

"*Kumme, dochder,* you look hungry. Noah, join us," she said, ignoring her husband's stern look.

"*Nee,* Elma. Go back in the *haus.* I haven't finished speaking with her." He flashed her a look to obey him, gave her a quick kiss on the cheek, ushering her back in the house.

Miranda watched her mother hesitate at the door, tears welling up in her eyes. She knew it was the last time she would see her mother for a very long time.

She clenched her jaw and pursed her lips to keep from sobbing out loud in front of her father. He had always been very stern, and she knew before even telling him anything, that he was not going to approve of her situation, and would likely not let her back in the house. She would stay strong and stifle her emotions.

She would not let him see her cry.

"I asked you a question, *dochder,*" he said more sternly. "Where's your *mann*?"

"I don't have one," Miranda said, her lower lip quivering.

"Who did this to you?" He asked, as he pointed to her abdomen.

She began to open her mouth, but Noah squeezed her hand. "I'm the *vadder,* and I take full responsibility. I intend to marry her."

"You will both get off my property this instant. "You leave at once! You're not *wilkume* here. You've shamed our *familye* and the community with this. You may not return until you have made a full confession and taken the baptism, and then we will have a *hochzich*—wedding."

Her mother rushed back through the door and pulled her daughter into her arms. "Please don't do this Silas! Please don't! She's our *dochder;* the one we prayed would return home."

"Not like this!" he said, motioning to her stomach in anger. "She's not to come to us with this sin hanging over her head, and I will not tolerate her sinful ways in my home."

"I'm going to marry her," Noah tried reasoning with him. "I give you my word. I had no idea she was pregnant, but now that I do, I take full responsibility. Please don't turn away your *dochder*."

"Let her stay," *Frau* Yoder cried, as she held her daughter tight.

"Go in the *haus*," he ordered his wife.

Then he looked at Noah. "When you're finished confessing to the Bishop, then she can return until the *hochzich*. Until then, it's as if I never knew you."

He turned and walked into the house, closing the door without looking back.

Miranda began to cry as she grabbed her suitcase, but Noah took it from her and put it back in his buggy. Then, he assisted her back into the seat. He climbed in next to her, and she turned to him, her eyes rimmed in red. "Why did you defend me like that? Why did you lie to my father and say you're my baby's father? Why did you tell him you would marry me?"

"Because I still love you!" He put his hand in hers. "Marry me, Miranda. Marry me, so I can fix this for you."

Chapter Six

It was clear even to him that she would not marry him. Not like this, and not for these reasons. He'd made a genuine offer, but it was clear that wasn't what she wanted or needed at the moment. She was all alone now with her father sending her away, and no matter how much he wanted to fix that, he had to stand back and be a friend and support person for her, and nothing more. Asking her to marry him had only put more pressure on her; even he could see that. He'd meant well, but now he wished he'd have kept his mouth shut. She was frightened, and he was more concerned than ever for her and the baby.

"I have nowhere to go now," she sobbed. "I don't know what to do, but I can't marry you just for the sake of being taken care of."

"Let's not worry about that right now. I'll take you back to my house, and I'll stay in the *Dawdi haus*. You can stay in the main house with Belinda until we can figure this out. Surely by that time Simon will have cooled off, and perhaps he'll sober up enough to help you."

"He isn't going to help, and spending time in jail is only going to make him angrier. He has no intention of helping me or the baby. He's been on a down-hill spiral ever since we left the community. It was as if, all of a sudden, he wasn't grounded anymore by his parents, and he could do as he pleased without consequence. Only problem is, there were plenty of consequences, and I'm the one who's having to deal with them. His drinking has gotten so out of control, I think it's best if I refuse to see him and move on with my life. I have a child to think of now. Instead of growing up, which most people do as they age, he's gone further and further back and he acts like a sixteen-year-old. I do not want that sort of person for a spouse because it'll be like I have two children. I've learned a lot of hard lessons while I was out there amongst the *Englisch*, and I realized that I should've never left the community. Curiosity got the better of me, and I wish I hadn't let it. Because of that, I'm in a big mess. On top of that, I lost you."

"You haven't lost me," he said gently. "I'm still here, and if you'll have me, I'd like to marry you—when you're ready."

She sighed as she watched the sun filtering through the wooded area that lined the roadway. For a flicker of a second, it took her back to the many buggy rides she and Noah had taken—back before she'd lost her innocence.

"I don't want you to marry me out of pity."

"It wouldn't be out of pity," he said. "I told you I still love you, and I meant that."

She turned and looked at him with her blue eyes that had dimmed. "How could you after what I've done? I've made a mess of everything. Seems kind of unfair that the only way I can survive is to get married, don't you agree?"

"I suppose so," he said as he clicked to the horse, getting him to a slow trot. "What will you do if you don't marry me?"

"I don't know since I can't work my job anymore in town. At least not until the baby gets a little older."

"You know you're always *wilkume* to stay with Belinda and me, and that'll give you a chance to save a little money. Since neither of us has taken the baptism, we won't be shunned by the community for having you there."

"The people in the community will still talk," she protested. "What will you say?"

"I'll tell them I'm the *boppli's vadder,* and they should keep their noses out of your business."

"I can't let you do that for my sake," she said sadly. "I've been enough trouble already."

The jostling of the buggy was making her a little queasy, but she tried breathing a little slower, hoping it would pass. It had been so long since she'd been in a buggy, it seemed funny to her that she'd forgotten such a detail.

"I already told you we'll always be friends, and you'll always be *wilkume,* and my original offer still stands. If—when you change your mind, you just let me know."

She smiled inwardly, feeling thankful she had the option of accepting his offer.

He steered the buggy into his own driveway and pulled up the lane. Belinda was waiting impatiently for him, both hands on her hips, and a scornful look in her eye.

"Where did you run off to? It seems every Monday you do this, and I haven't said anything until now, but right now, I can't get the gas stove lit. I needed your help getting it lit, and now the meal is going to be late because you weren't here. Where exactly do you go?"

Belinda watched as Miranda exited the buggy, her gaze falling to her swelled abdomen.

"Miranda?" Belinda asked, feeling the hair on the back of her neck stand on end.

Something was amiss, but she wasn't certain she was looking forward to the answer.

"Where's your *mann*, and why are you here with my *brudder*?"

"She hasn't got a husband, Belinda. Mind your own business," Noah snapped at her.

"This *is* my business if you're bringing your old girlfriend into *mei haus*."

Noah pointed to the house. "That's just as much my *haus* as it is yours, and she's going to be staying there with you for a while."

"Where's the *vadder* of her *boppli*?"

Noah was growing weary of his sister's overabundance of questions.

"I'm the *boppli's vadder*," he said without blinking an eye.

She sucked in her breath. "But that can't be! What would *mamm* and *dat* say about this?"

"It doesn't matter what they would say, because they aren't here to say it, and I'd appreciate it if you'd keep your comments on the subject to yourself."

"If you're that *boppli's vadder*, why haven't you married her?"

"Because I just found out about it myself today," he said.

He was digging himself in deeper, but he felt the need to protect Miranda's already soiled reputation.

"I asked her to marry me, and she turned me down. So she'll be staying in the main *haus* with you, and I'll be sleeping in the *dawdi haus.* At least until she accepts my proposal."

"Who said I was going to accept?" Miranda asked, annoyance in her tone.

"You will," he said with confidence. "Why wouldn't you? I love you, and that's my *boppli* you're carrying!"

His sister pressed her hands to her hips. "Noah, you and I both know that isn't true, so you might as well tell me who it is!"

"I already told you, Belinda, that *boppli* is mine, and I don't want to hear another word about it."

"Are the two of you planning on living here once you're married?"

"*Nee!*" he said sternly. "So you might want to start fishing around for a *mann* for yourself so you don't have to live here alone."

"That's *narrish!* I can't just *find* myself a *mann*," she said angrily. "It's not that easy. I'm too old!"

"How do you figure? I went into town, and look at me. I've got a *fraa* and a *boppli* all in one day!"

She pursed her lips. "I *knew* that *boppli* wasn't yours!"

He looked at Miranda, and then back at his sister. "It will be!"

Chapter Seven

After she settled Miranda into one of the rooms upstairs, Belinda went downstairs where Noah was sitting in the kitchen, a cup of coffee resting on the table, his hands cupped around it.

"You're going to get us both shunned; you know that, right?"

"*Nee,* that won't happen since neither of us has taken the baptism."

"I suppose you're right about that little *brudder;* we're practically shunned already."

"We still attend church; we just don't participate in much of the other things. Since *mamm* and *dat* died, they haven't pushed us to take the baptism, and they've been there for us. I guess you could say we have the best of both worlds."

Belinda poured herself a cup of coffee and sat across from her brother. It had been a long day, and she needed to sit for a minute before tackling the chore of washing dishes.

"Seeing Miranda in the condition she's in, I'd have to say I'm glad you didn't go that day when you dropped them off in town."

"Seeing her makes me wish more than ever that I'd gone with her that day, or begged her to stay! How did you know that's what I was doing that day?"

"You forget *brudder,* that I was blessed with *mamm's* instincts about these things. I also know that you've been going off every Monday hoping to find her again. Now that you did, and given the condition she's in, do you really plan to marry her?"

"I do. That is, if she'll have me."

"You already asked her? I thought you were joking! What did she say? I'm guessing the answer was no."

She reached for the bowl of sugar in the center of the table and dropped another spoonful in her coffee.

"You guessed that right," he said with a sigh. "But I think she just needs some time."

She stirred the coffee, the spoon clinking against the inside of the cup.

"By the way," she said, tapping the spoon against the edge of the cup and setting it on the saucer. "What happened to her face?"

"When I found her, the *boppli's vadder* was smacking her around."

Belinda gasped. "Is she okay?"

"*Jah,* but I'm afraid it shook me up more than it did her."

She sipped her coffee. "What do you mean?"

"It was Simon who hit her. Simon is the *boppli's vadder.*"

Belinda leaned back in the chair and whispered a little prayer. "*Gott help her.*"

She leaned back up and searched her brother's eyes. "You know this for sure that he's the *vadder*?"

"*Jah,*" he admitted to them living together, and she admitted he's the *vadder*. He went to jail for hitting her. That's where he is now."

She slurped the last of her coffee. "All that, and you still want to marry her?"

"*Jah,* but it makes me want to marry her even more. I wish I would have begged her not to go that day when I dropped her and Simon off in town. I wish I could change a lot of things about that day."

"Such as going with them?" Belinda asked. She jumped up and grabbed her cup, and poured herself another cup of coffee, even though she worried it wouldn't do anything to calm her nerves.

He stared out the window for a moment, watching a couple of birds taking a dip in the bird-bath in his *mamm's* flowerbed. She'd loved those flowers. Belinda had cared for them like they were her little children ever since their parents had died. Life was too precious, and the ones you love could slip away too easily. It was what inspired him to propose to Miranda. He didn't want to lose her again; he knew his heart couldn't bear the strain of breaking again.

"As a matter of fact, I'm glad I stayed. I don't wish that I would have gone with them; I used to. But I wish that I would have done something, anything, to talk them out of going in the first place. It's a hard lesson that they've both had to learn, and the hardest part is ahead of both of them. Even if she does marry me, Simon will still be in our lives since he's the *vadder*, and it'll be tough on all of us because I'm not sure that he'll ever get over the bitterness. You should've seen the look in his eyes when they took him off to jail. What he doesn't understand is that I feel somewhat responsible because I was his friend, and I feel like I let him down. I let them both down. I should have tried harder to convince them to stay."

"They made their own choices. You're not responsible."

He shook his head. "You're wrong. I should have tried harder to talk them out of going, but I didn't. I was a coward; afraid they would resent me if I begged them to stay. Now I think they both resent me for letting them go, and I feel so bad for both of them."

She slurped at her coffee, once again finding the bottom of the cup. "What about Miranda? Regardless of how her *boppli* came into this world, it's still a blessing from *Gott.*"

He stood and went to the kitchen window, leaning against the counter and staring out at the barn. He and Miranda had shared many stolen kisses in that barn. She would often sneak over and surprise him in the wee hours of the morning and kept him company while he did his chores.

"I know the *boppli* is a blessing, and that's what makes it so hard to regret that part of it more than anything. If only I'd been looking more serious about the marriage proposal. All she wanted was for me to ask her to stay, and I wouldn't. Because of that I lost her, and I've regretted it every day since. But the *boppli* is a blessing, so I suppose *Gott* allowed this. Knowing that makes it easier to want to marry her."

Belinda crossed the room and stood by the window with him, remembering her days in the loft of the barn with Seth; all the plans they'd made that had never come to pass. "Sometimes, little *brudder,* we have to swallow our regrets and move on. You have a real possibility of a future with her; you should do everything in your power to prevent her slipping away from you a second time. Don't push her too fast or you may lose her again. Make her feel safe, and love her. Leave the rest to *Gott.*"

"I'm certainly going to try," Noah said. A crack of thunder interrupted their conversation, and she looked out at the dark sky through the kitchen window.

"*Ach,*" she said, jumping at the second rumble that rattled the windows. "I forgot I have wash on the line, and I need to get it down before the rain hits."

Noah headed for the door, ready to help without grumbling for a change, realizing the problems with his friends had opened his eyes to just how lucky he was in his current situation.

"Let's go *schweschder;* we have laundry to take care of."

Chapter Eight

Miranda stepped onto the front porch, where she found Belinda and Noah sitting on the wicker rocking chairs that reminded her of home. Light rain drizzled from the sky and blew around in waves in such a way that if one didn't know any better, it could almost look like snow. The dark sky lit up frequently with lightning that scattered across the sky against the backdrop of the rain. A low, deep rumble would follow, and the wind would pick up momentarily.

She shivered, standing there for a moment, remembering a similar night on this very porch nearly a year ago. She and Noah had made plans that night; plans they thought would result in a better future than living the slow life in the Amish community. They craved the excitement of the *Englisch* world, and daydreamed a little too much that night. She realized now that it had been just enough to talk Noah *out* of going instead of talking him into running away with her the way she'd hoped. She knew he'd been riding the fence, not wanting to leave his sister behind, and in the end, he'd held fast to his responsibility to her. That was all water under the bridge now, and there was nothing she could do to turn back the hands of time.

It had been a long winter without him, and an even longer summer without her time with him on this porch. Another season was nearly behind them, and it saddened Miranda that their childhood days were over.

Belinda rose from her chair when she noticed Miranda's hesitancy, and gestured for her to take her place Next to Noah.

"*wie gehts?*" she asked politely.

"I'm feeling better, *danki.*" The word felt foreign to Miranda, who'd spent the past year trying her best to fit into the *Englisch* world, that she'd forgotten how much more comfortable it could be here in this place where no one pretended.

"I'll get some lemonade while the two of you talk." She left without another word, and Miranda slowly sank into the wicker rocking chair beside Noah.

"Did you sleep well?" he asked. "I thought you might sleep through the night."

"Jah, danki, I did. But I don't feel very rested. Perhaps because I only slept for a few hours, or because I shouldn't have accepted the second piece of *snitz* pie that Belinda offered me. Honestly, I'm betting it's the stress."

"It's probably the stress," he offered. "Things will get better with time. I promise."

"I wish I could believe a promise like that," she said rolling her hand over her swelling abdomen. "But with the wee one coming along any day now, I'm a little weary in my faith."

He thought of his own faith, and how much it had wavered over the long months while Miranda was separated from him. He'd gone from angry, to questioning, and then to feeling hopeless.

"I'm sure *Gott* understands that." He rested his hand on hers, hoping it would bring her comfort.

"You know," she said. "It seems like a whole lifetime ago that we last sat on the porch together. I've missed this."

He nodded and squeezed her hand. "It does seem like it's been forever since we were here that night. I've missed you too."

"I was so angry with you that night."

He turned to her, searching her eyes for answers, but found none.

"Why were you angry with me?"

She sighed. "Because I knew, just as sure as we're sitting here right now, that you didn't intend to go. Your heart was here, and I knew you wouldn't leave Belinda or this farm—or your responsibility. It angered me. It was the reason I gave in to

Simon that night. I know that's no excuse, but I was still so angry with you. Especially since I'd seen you in town every Monday since that day you dropped us off. You were there, but you weren't really there. You weren't with me where I needed you to be—in the *Englisch* world, and I resented you for it. I would watch you every Monday; I'd sit across the street at the diner, and I'd watch you come into town, watch you sit at the fountain and brood, and then I'd watch you leave. I knew part of you was beating yourself up for your decision, but I just couldn't bring myself to step outside the diner, crossing the street, and falling into your arms, the way I'd imagined it so many times."

"Why didn't you come talk to me?" he asked. "At that point I would've begged you to come home with me."

"That night when we sat on the porch, I wanted you to beg me to stay, but you didn't, and it hurt me deeply. I guess I couldn't let go of that hurt."

He pulled her hand to his face and kissed the back of it lovingly. "You wanted me to ask you to stay?" he asked. "Why didn't you just say so?"

She enjoyed the tingling from his kiss that traveled all the way up her arm. "I didn't want to embarrass myself in case I was wrong about how you were feeling. I was so confused and mixed up myself; I didn't know what to think."

He rocked gently in the wicker rocker, listening to the rain, and catching intermittent glimpses of her when the lightning lit up the night sky.

"Why didn't things work out between you and Simon?"

"He was too busy being rebellious, and I was on the rebound from losing you. Like I said, I was angry with you, and being with him might have been a way of lashing out at you. I can't really say for sure because I just couldn't forgive you for not asking me to stay, and for not going with me. Either way, I would've been happy. All I wanted was to be with you, either here or there, but now that I've been there all I wanted the whole time was to be back here with you."

She began to sob, her shoulders shaking lightly.

He knelt down before her and pulled her close. "I wish you would've said something. I wish I could take it all back, and we could turn back the hands of time; or start over again. I love you; I've missed you so much, I've ached. I've dreamt of the moment I'd hold you again so many times, I feared it would never happen, yet here you are. We've wasted so much time that we could've been together. Let's not waste another minute of it. I'm terrified of losing you again. Won't you marry me?"

Her sobs increased, and she couldn't bear to torture either of them any longer.

"It's too late for all of that now," she whispered.

Chapter Nine

As hard as it was for him, Noah decided to take his sister's advice, and give Miranda some space. Despite his need to fix everything for her, he knew there were things she needed to fix for herself before she could give him an answer. He would be there for her no matter what, even if it meant she went back to Simon when all was said and done, but he prayed that would not happen.

The last thing he wanted to do was push her away even further than he had the first time. If he lost her now, he might never get her back. He would accept the chance that God had dropped her in his lap, and be patient and wait on the Lord to change her heart.

She leaned her head on his shoulder, and though he was tempted to put his arm around her and pull her close, he resisted the urge. He wanted so much for things to be perfect between the two of them, but the baby she was carrying would be the deciding factor.

If she accepted his offer of marriage and decided to let him raise her child as his own, then all would be fine. If not, it might forever be between them, and Simon could become a thorn in both their sides. If Simon was truly rejecting of this baby, he would have no problems raising it. But if Simon showed the slightest bit interested, he would have an obligation to keep him in the child's life even if he wasn't raising him.

No matter how disappointed he was with Simon, he was still the baby's true father, and for that reason, he would make every effort not to put his own desires for Miranda above his friend's need to be in his child's life.

Noah turned his head, burying his nose in her hair. It smelled of lilacs and fresh ginger. It was a scent he'd missed so much. He'd missed everything about her, and he was close to getting her back, he feared everything about it. He knew if he wasn't careful, his heart would get broken again, but he prayed God would spare him the heartbreak this time around. He fully believed that God had put Miranda back in his path for a reason and that he'd been at the park today for the sole purpose of bringing her back home—back into his life. He also believed God knew that she needed him just as much as he needed her.

"*Ach,*" she said, as she jumped, placing her hand to her abdomen.

"What's wrong?" Noah asked in a panic.

She grabbed his hand and gently placed it on her abdomen. "Do you feel that?" she asked

"*Jah,* what is that?"

"That," she said with a smile "is your *boppli* kicking."

His smile widened. "*Mei boppli*, huh?"

"I suppose it is; if you really wanted it to be."

"Are you sure?" he asked.

"*Jah*," she said with a smile. "I've been dreaming of it for so long, the very thought of it coming true scared me. But I can't keep lying to myself anymore about how I feel toward you. I've never stopped loving you, and I've missed you more than you can know."

"Probably not as much as I've missed you. But we're together now, and that's all that matters."

"Can you really raise this *boppli* with me, even though it isn't yours?"

"Simon is my best friend, and I was going to marry you once. I don't see any reason I shouldn't still marry you. I don't have any problem raising the *boppli* with you. It's a part of my best friend and the woman I love. I will love it like it was my own."

He pulled her into his arms, unable to hold back his love for her any longer. His lips met hers in a whirlwind of passion, but he couldn't hold back any longer. His lips were soft and yielding, yet strong.

She parted her lips and allowed him to kiss her freely. She still loved him; she couldn't help herself. Though her mistake had changed things for them, it had not changed their hearts. They would never be the same people, but their love had endured.

She'd missed his strong arms around her. How could she have traded this feeling for the *Englisch* world outside the safety of the community?

He continued to kiss her, but his thoughts drifted. He could easily forgive her mistake. After all, he'd let her go, and she'd been free to live her life. Simon, on the other hand, was going to be tough to forgive. His actions of violence toward Miranda were shocking, at the very least, and had caused him to hit his lifetime friend.

Miranda tipped Noah's chin, looking him in the eye. "You stopped kissing me, and you have a faraway look in your eyes."

He forced a weak smile. "I'm sorry. I was thinking about Simon."

Her expression showed disappointment. "That's not what I want you thinking about when I'm kissing you!"

"It wasn't like that!" He laughed at her comment.

She crossed her arms over her belly. "I don't ever want to see him again as long as I live!"

"That's a little harsh, don't you think? I know he hit you—and me too, but we should forgive him."

"I'm not sure I'll ever be able to do that," she admitted.

He wanted so much to be strong for her, but a part of him felt the same way she did. His only choice was to lead by example. It was his duty to her as her husband-to-be. He would soon be the spiritual head over her and the child, and it was up to him to keep them on the straight and narrow path. God had brought them together, and Noah would let no man tear them asunder—especially not Simon.

Chapter Ten

Noah took a second look at Belinda when she entered the barn. "What are you all dressed up in your Sunday dress for?"

He watched his sister's face turn several shades of red, while she cast her eyes down at the floor of the barn.

"I need you to hitch up the buggy for me. I'm going over to the Troyer *haus* to stay with his *kinner* for a while. He asked me after church on Sunday."

"Are you sweet on the Widower Troyer?" Noah teased.

"Nee," she said with a furrowed brow. "I'm watching his *kinner,* nothing more. I watch his *kinner* all the time; you know that."

"*Jah,* but you never wear your Sunday dress to do that. Every other time you go over there, you wear your work dress because those *kinner* are a handful. If you're not sweet on him, why are you so dressed up?"

She pursed her lips. "If you must know, he's hinted to me several times recently that he was still interested in marrying me, but I couldn't do that when I knew how tough this last year has been for you. You needed me to take care of you, so I turned him down. Now that you'll be marrying Miranda, you won't want me around. I figured I'd accept his proposal when I went over there today."

Noah felt poorly. He'd rushed into everything so fast with Miranda, that he must have hurt Belinda's feelings with his announcement.

"I didn't mean what I said to you yesterday," he said. "I was only teasing when I told you that you needed to find yourself a *mann. Ach,* don't take that seriously. My marrying Miranda isn't going to change things here. We can live in the *dawdi haus* until I can get our cousins to help me build a new *haus.* On the other hand, if you love Josiah Troyer, you should move on with your life and stop hiding behind me to keep from living your life. You should have married him a couple of years ago when he first asked you when his mourning period ended."

"You knew about that?"

Noah laughed. "You think the women in the community are the only ones who talk? The only reason I didn't say anything was because I didn't think you were interested in him. I thought you were still pining for Seth. But I realized, now that I've grown up a little, that you couldn't leave me any more than I could leave you. If you want to marry him, you have my blessing. He's a *gut mann,* and he'll make a fine husband."

He's strong and handsome, too, she thought.

She smiled and pulled her brother into a hug. "*Danki!* I pray I'm not too late to accept his offer of marriage."

"Amen!" Noah said. "Let me get the buggy for you. While you wait, why don't you go put some of those cookies and muffins you made into a basket, and take them with you?"

"What for?"

"The best way to get a husband is to feed him!"

She giggled, and ran into the house to do exactly as her brother told her to do. She felt giddy as she put together the baked goods. She never imagined she could ever feel happy again, but the thought of marrying Josiah made her feel like a young girl in love. She'd been denying her feelings for so long, it felt liberating to finally be able to admit them—to herself, and to her brother.

~~~~

Belinda tied up her buggy under the shade tree in Josiah's driveway, noting that the other buggy looked a lot like the new buggy Rachel Yoder had gotten after her husband had died last year, when a car collided with his buggy on U.S. 20, near the *Essenhaus*.

What would Rachel be doing here? She asked herself.

She stepped onto the porch, and looked out into the yard, spotting Josiah's daughter, Eva, pushing Rachel's daughter, Faith, on the tire swing. When Eva saw her on the porch, she ran to greet her, leaving Faith to stop the swing by herself. She hopped up on the porch, Faith running toward them.

"Faith is going to stay here and play with me today while her *mamm* goes for a picnic with *mei dat!*"

Belinda felt her heart sink to her feet, but tried her best not to show her disappointment. Josiah was her last hope to keep from being a spinster, and she truly loved him. Now, she had become nothing more than a caregiver to him so he could court another woman. Why was it that God had allowed her to get her hopes up, only to let her heart be crushed twice in her lifetime?

The front door swung open and Rachel greeted her wearing a new blue dress. Her mourning clothes had been put away, perhaps before their time. Had it been a year already?

She bit her lip to keep the tears from welling up in her eyes when Josiah joined Rachel at the door. She suddenly felt like a fool for having worn her best dress. Surely Rachel would notice she wasn't wearing the sort of dress normally worn for such a chore as watching *kinner*. There would be chores like cooking involved, and the dress she had on was not practical. Should she try making an excuse to save herself embarrassment?

"What's in the basket?" seven-year-old Eva asked as she pulled on it.

Belinda had forgotten about the basket of baked-goods she'd brought for Josiah, and now felt like an even bigger fool.

"I brought you and your *brudder* some cookies," she said, hoping to save-face.

The little one cheered and snatched it from her hands and ran into the house, Faith on her heels.

"I hope you don't mind if we leave Faith here with you today, too," Josiah said to Belinda.

"*Nee,*" she said, biting her lip again. "It will do Eva *gut* to have a friend here to play with. That way Caleb can beat me at a couple rounds of checkers."

She forced a smile when Caleb came running out with a cookie in his mouth. "Did I hear you say checkers?" he asked, spitting crumbs onto the porch.

She bit her bottom lip, knowing these little ones would never be hers. She mourned the loss of them already.

She took his hand and allowed him to lead her into the house. Perhaps after Josiah married Rachel, they would still ask her to watch the children.

Who was she fooling? They would be a family, and they wouldn't need her anymore, and neither would the children. They would have a new mother, and Belinda would never have any of her own.

"*Danki,*" she heard Rachel say behind her. "We'll be a few hours at least."

She turned slowly, seeing the picnic basket in Josiah's hand, Rachel tucking her arm in the crook of his arm as they exited the house.

Belinda tried to tell herself it didn't matter, and that she could be happy for Rachel, but she just couldn't. Suddenly, she felt the same as she had when Seth had run off with Priscilla. The only difference was that she and Rachel were not as close as she had been with Priscilla. It didn't keep her from seething with jealousy.

Caleb brought the checkers down from the shelf and tucked his hand in hers, leading her out to the front porch. Eva and Faith followed, cookies shoved in their hands.

"Miss Belinda," Eva asked. "Will you ask *mei dat* to marry Faith's *mamm* so we can be *schweschders?*"

Belinda bit her bottom lip and forced a smile. It wasn't too long ago that Eva was begging Belinda to be her new *mamm.*

"I still want *you* to be *mei mamm,* but I want a *schweschder* too!"

Belinda couldn't help but smile because of Eva's childish comment. *"Ach,* your *dat* can only marry one person, and that person is up to him to decide."

Her bottom lip puffed out. "I was afraid you'd say that."

The two girls ran back to the tire swing, and Belinda walked over to the pair of wooden rockers that Josiah had built, and lowered herself into the one facing the girls so she could keep an eye on them. Caleb had set up the checkers on the table between the rockers, and sat down, ready to play.

~~~

Belinda rushed into the house, unable to stifle the tears any longer. She'd hastily begged Noah to put away her horse and the buggy, but not before he tried to question her about how things had gone with Josiah. Instead of answering him, she excused herself and ran into the house before she burst into tears in front of him. The last thing she wanted was to suffer even more humiliation than she already had.

Once she was safely in her room with the door closed, she flung herself over her bed and cried into her pillow, muffling the sobs that just wouldn't stop. Several minutes went by before a light knock at her door caused her to quiet herself. She sat up on the bed, wiping her eyes, and looking in the mirror. There would be no hiding her red-rimmed eyes from whoever was on the other end of that knock.

"*Jah?*" she said with a shaky voice.

"The Widower Troyer is here to see you," Miranda's soft voice announced through the door.

Panic filled Belinda. How was she going to face him when he'd obviously come to break the news that he would be marrying Rachel?

Chapter Eleven

"Just a minute," Belinda called through the door.

She looked into the mirror, realizing she'd have to open the door, and there would be no hiding her red face and puffy eyes from Miranda.

She wished she didn't even have to leave her room, feeling extremely confused as to why Josiah had followed her home.

She couldn't go to him looking like this; she knew she would rather Miranda wouldn't see her either, but there was no getting around it. As long as the girl didn't ask for an explanation, Belinda wouldn't break down again before having to greet Josiah. If she had her way, she would have Miranda make an excuse for her and refuse to see him, but she hadn't been brought up to be rude. No matter how painful it would be to face him, she knew it was best to get it over with so she could get on with her life. The sooner she accepted she would be a spinster for the rest of her life, the easier it would be on her. It was not going to be easy to give up her hope of being a mother and a wife, but she had only herself to blame. She'd put off answering the widower for too long, and now she would have to suffer the consequences.

The least she could do would be to face him and let him speak his peace. She owed him that much.

It's hard to mourn the loss of something you never had, she told herself, hoping it would make her feel better.

It didn't.

She took in a deep breath and opened the door. Miranda stood there with a sad smile on her face and her arms outstretched. Belinda collapsed into her arms and sobbed for only a minute.

"I'm so sorry for whatever is troubling you," she said as she smoothed Belinda's stray hairs that had come loose from her prayer *kapp*. "But you have a very handsome *mann* waiting for you, and he's brought you flowers!"

"Likely a peace-offering!" Belinda said, sniffling.

"It didn't look like a peace-offering to me!" she said. "He looked like a *mann* who was coming to court."

"I wish that were true," Belinda said as she walked into the bathroom. "When I went there today, I intended to accept his offer of marriage, but he took Rachel Yoder for a picnic, and left me to stay with both their *kinner*. I haven't felt this humiliated since Seth ran off with my best friend, Priscilla!"

She splashed cold water on her face, hoping it would take away the redness, but it only made it worse.

"You've got it all wrong, Belinda!" she said with a kind smile. "Today was the anniversary of the death of Rachel's husband—he was my cousin. The widower Troyer was his good friend, and so he took Rachel back to the site where he died, and the two of them had a picnic in his honor as a way to say goodbye to him. That's all there was to it. It was completely innocent."

Belinda looked up from the sink and turned off the water. "How do you know this?"

"I saw her in town earlier this morning when I went with Noah to get some things to fix the barn door, and she told me all about it. She was so grateful that you would be staying with the children because she wanted to spare Faith from anymore heartache over her father's death."

Belinda's heart beat hard and fast at the news, and a smile returned to her face. Was it possible that Josiah was here to call on her the way Miranda said? It was too scary to hope for such a thing.

"Tell him I'll be down in a minute," she said. "I'd like to give my face a minute to calm down and not be so red."

She smiled at Belinda. "I understand. I'll tell him."

When Miranda went downstairs, Belinda said a prayer, asking God to give her strength to endure an answer of "no", if that was what it was to be, or the grace and humility to accept a "yes" if that was His Will.

She washed her face one last time, and then took a deep breath, knowing that no matter how her talk ended with Josiah, it would be God's Will for her life, and she would accept it.

Taking another deep breath, she descended slowly down the stairs. In her father's chair near the fireplace, Josiah sat with a bouquet of wild flowers in his hand. He stood and looked at her as she entered the room. His smile warmed her already pink cheeks, his kind, brown eyes inviting her to trust him.

She closed the space between them, intending to sit in the chair across from him, but he remained standing as he greeted her.

"I didn't get a chance to thank you for staying with the *kinner*," he said as he handed her the bouquet.

"*Danki* for the flowers, but you didn't have to come all this way just to say that."

"I didn't come over here just to say that," he admitted. "You left before I had the chance to tell you that I arranged to have Rachel stay with the *kinner* so you and I could take a buggy ride. That is, if you're finally open to being courted by me."

Her heart thumped hard and fast. She never took him for one of those men who would see more than one woman at a time; so perhaps, there was some truth to what Miranda had told her a few minutes ago.

He asked Rachel to stay with the kinner so he could take me for a buggy ride? I'd be a fool to turn down this handsome mann twice!

His smiling, hopeful expression spoke of his sincerity.

"*Jah,*" she said with a smile. "Would you like to take a thermos full of *kaffi* along with us?"

"Do you have any of those cookies left?" he asked with a smile. "The *kinner* ate every one of them, and I miss those melt-in-your-mouth cookies!"

"*Jah,* I'll bring some!" she said, the pitch to her voice showing her excitement. "Let me tell Noah I'll be leaving."

"I already spoke to him. When I saw him in town this morning, I asked him permission to court you, so he knew I would be asking you for a buggy ride this evening."

Belinda sucked in her breath. "He did?"

"He didn't expect you home this early. He thought you'd be taking the buggy ride as soon as Rachel and I got back from the memorial we had for her husband, Levi. He told me you'd come home upset and thought I'd changed my mind. You didn't think Rachel and I were out courting, did you?"

Her face heated at his question. "*Nee,*" she said, trying to hide her embarrassment. "Why don't I hurry and get the *kaffi* and cookies ready so we can go."

He smiled, letting it go, realizing that she must have thought that very thing, but didn't want to tell him. He had to admit, the thought of her being jealous flattered him.

Chapter Twelve

Miranda leaned against the kitchen counter, her breath catching in her throat when another pain assaulted her. She'd been having the pains since the wee hours of the morning, and they'd become nearly unbearable.

She was the only one in the house, and she was beginning to get a little frightened. With Belinda out for a buggy ride with Josiah, and Noah out on the acreage somewhere, she had no idea where help would come from if she should really need it.

A knock at the back door startled her.

Taking a deep breath, she wiped the sweat from her brow and went to the door, slowly, fearing if she hurried, the extreme pain would return.

Her heart skipped a beat when she opened the door to her mother, who stood with a welcoming smile and a basket of canned peaches.

Miranda's hand went instinctively to her abdomen, feeling self-conscious about it in front of her mother.

"May I come in, Miranda," her mother asked. "I'd like to visit with you for a minute."

"*Jah,*" she said, finding her voice. "Does *dat* know you're here?"

Her eyes cast downward. "*Nee,* I'm afraid he's not ready to accept this."

Tears welled up in Miranda's eyes. "I don't want him to be *shemt*—ashamed of me."

She put a hand under her daughter's chin and raised it just enough until their eyes met. "He's not *shemt* of you. He's getting on in years, and he's worried he won't have the support of the community when he needs it most. He doesn't know any other way, and we don't have any money saved—at least not much to speak of. He's afraid of getting shunned."

Miranda could understand that—given her present condition.

"Sit down, *mamm,* and I'll get us some *kaffi.*"

Her mother sat down at the table in the kitchen, while Miranda went to the gas stove to pour them a cup of coffee. Pain radiated from her back, to her abdomen with such force, it nearly took her breath away. She paused at the stove, bracing herself for the wave of pain, knowing it would get worse before it would get better.

Her mother rushed to her side. "Are you alright, *dochder?*"

"*Jah,*" she said through gritted teeth. "It's nothing."

"*Kumme,* sit down." Elma guided her daughter to a chair at the table. "You need to breathe slowly. Don't breathe like that if you can help it, or you might faint."

Her mother showed her how to breathe to help ease the pains.

"That was *gut!*" her mother said. "How often have the pains been coming? When did they start?"

"They woke me up this morning—when the sun was coming up. They've been coming about every ten minutes, but these last few were faster."

"Where's Noah?"

"He's outside," Miranda groaned, another pain taking her by surprise. "I'm not sure where."

Elma positioned herself in front of Miranda. "I need you to breathe slowly in through your mouth and out through your nose."

Miranda blew out a ragged breath as slowly as she could, a stifled cry escaping with it. "I'm scared, *mamm*. I think something's wrong. I'm in a lot of pain."

Her mother smiled, and wiped her daughter's brow with the dishtowel. "There's nothing to be afraid of; I'm here with you, and I won't leave you. Everything seems to be just fine. Your wee one is on its way, ain't it so?"

Miranda started to cry happy tears. "You'll really stay with me?"

Elma pulled her into a hug. "I won't leave you! You're going to have a wee one of your own, and I wouldn't miss such an important time for you."

She groaned against another pain. They were less than two minutes apart.

"What about *dat?*" she asked once the pain subsided.

"Let me worry about your *dat.* You concentrate on your *boppli.*"

She cried out in pain, squeezing her eyes closed and bearing down. "I need my doctor!" she screamed. "I need to go to the hospital."

Elma looked at her daughter. She'd become *Englisch.* Was she prepared to let her go to a world she knew nothing about? It seemed to be Miranda's choice.

"Do you have a phone?" she asked.

She pointed to the counter. "It's over there. I was going to call a cab before you showed up, but now, I think I need an ambulance."

Elma grabbed the phone and brought it to Miranda. "I don't know how to work it. Tell me what to do."

She took the phone from her mother, and dialed in 911, and then handed it to her. "Tell the person you need an ambulance for me. Give them the address here. Tell them to hurry!"

Noah walked in the door, and seeing Miranda in the shape she was in, rushed to her side.

"I heard you crying from the barn," he said. Wiping her cheeks and pulling her into his arms. "Let's get you more comfortable."

He picked her up and took her to the room that used to belong to his parents. Belinda had turned it into a guest room years ago, and had settled Miranda in the room so she wouldn't have to navigate the stairs.

Once he placed her on the bed, he waited for her mother to get off the phone. "Are you staying here to help?"

"*Jah,*" she said. "Get me some extra sheets and towels. I'm also going to need some washed sewing sheers and a spool of thread."

"What about the ambulance?"

"I don't think they're going to make it in time," she said. "Hurry and get what I asked you for."

Noah went to his sister's sewing machine in the living room and picked up a pair of sheers from the table, and removed the thread from the top of the machine. At the kitchen sink, he washed the scissors, and then grabbed fresh linens from the closet in the hall.

He paused at the door to the bedroom, listening to Miranda's cries. His intention was to wait until she quieted down between contractions, but the sound of the back door swinging open sent him back to the kitchen.

Silas Yoder stood with his feet squared on the linoleum tiles, hands on his hips, and a furrow to his dark brow. His black felt hat was tilted down over his eyes, but Noah could see anger in his expression.

A cry from the other room made the older man raise his eyebrows and glare at Noah. "Where's *mei fraa?*"

Noah pointed to the direction of the cries. "She's in there with your *dochder.* She's having her *boppli.*"

He could tell by the angered look on his face that *Frau* Yoder had not told her husband she was coming over here.

"Get *mei fraa,*" he said sternly. "I've come to take her home."

Chapter Thirteen

Miranda's screams pierced the silence in the kitchen between the two men. Silas could feel his heart twisting with worry for his daughter. He was caught between his fear of staying, and his responsibility and love for his child.

Another scream rent the air, followed by the cries of a newborn.

Noah wasn't going to stand there with the stubborn man any longer while he made up his mind if he would do the right thing or not.

"You can leave or stay, it's up to you, but I'm going in there and seeing my new *boppli.*"

Noah left Silas in the kitchen, and rushed to the bedroom, knowing Elma would need the sheers to cut the cord.

He tossed the things onto the foot of the bed when he entered the room where Miranda was draped in sheets. The infant resting in the crook of her arm whimpered, but the smile on her face was strong and proud. Her golden hair was damp, and loose from her prayer *kapp,* her pink cheeks glistened with light perspiration.

"*Kumme,* Noah; meet your son," Miranda said.

His heart swelled with pride. His son. No words could describe the elation he felt at this moment, and he was certain the smile on his face would not leave him as he gazed upon the infant in her arms.

Miranda's mother tied the cord and cut it, and then rewrapped the crying baby to keep him warm.

"You have a fine boy there, Noah," she said to him.

He turned to her, unable to thank her enough for being here for her daughter. "You have a fine grandson," he said to her.

"*Gott* has surely blessed us this day, ain't it so?"

Noah bent to kiss Miranda and the baby.

A son. He had a son.

What would Simon think about him? Would he want the boy for himself?

Noah shook off the worry for the time-being. His father had always told him not to borrow trouble, and here he was doing exactly that.

He gazed lovingly at the two of them, wondering what he had done to make God shine upon him the way he was now. He would accept the calling God had put on him, and he would protect Miranda and…what would they call the baby?

"Have you picked out a name?" he asked, wondering if she would name him after Simon.

A knock at the door interrupted them momentarily. Belinda stood there with a very humble-looking Silas Yoder.

"May we come in and see the *boppli?*"

"Jah," Miranda said with a wide smile.

Her father came near the head of the bed and smiled nervously at his daughter.

"Would you like to hold your grandson?" she asked. "I'd like to name him Silas, if it pleases you, *Dat.*"

"Jah," he said, taking the baby in his arms. "I think that's a fine name for him."

Silas held his namesake. After having only one child—a daughter, he finally had a boy in the family to help carry on his bloodline. He would be a proud grandfather, and teach him all he needed to know about farming. At least he'd stand beside his own father and help teach him the Amish ways.

He looked over at his wife of twenty-five years, thinking she'd never looked lovelier. She'd defied his stubborn pride for once and helped to bring his grandson safely into the world, and he couldn't love her more for it.

Off in the distance, sirens wailed, but they were too late. This new addition to his family had been brought into the world in the traditional Amish way, and that was the way he would be raised.

Silas intended to make sure of it.

Chapter Fourteen

Miranda rolled over in her sleepy state and put her hand on little Silas in his cradle—the very cradle she had slept in as an infant. Her parents had given it to her, along with the little white, linen gowns that had belonged to her. The quilt her mother had made for her was probably the biggest surprise in all of the gifts they'd bestowed upon her. Elma had saved a dowry for her, and those items were among the many things she'd been given to set up her new life with Noah as a married woman and mother.

Baby Silas arched his back and squeaked, a sure sign he was ready for his morning feeding. She sat up and smiled at her three-day-old infant son.

"Today is the day you get a *vadder*," she whispered to him.

It was her wedding day.

Her parents had agreed a small garden wedding between the main house and the *dawdi haus* on Noah's property was the best place for the wedding. They'd even agreed that since neither she, nor Noah had yet taken the baptism, it was best not to wait, especially since neither of them had yet made up their minds if they would even join the church. In the end, they all decided to have the Mennonite preacher perform the ceremony.

Birds chirped outside the bedroom window, alerting her that the sun was on its way up.

In the dim twilight, she changed her baby and sat down in the rocking chair—also a gift from her parents—and put her baby to her breast. She looked down at his little face, still full of wonder at the wee one God had blessed her with. He was truly perfect in every way.

She'd gotten up a few times in the night, giddy over her wedding. Belinda had stayed up into the late hours sewing Miranda a blue dress for her wedding today, and she was excited. She was getting a sister—something she'd wanted all her life.

Outside her window, she could see her husband-to-be headed for the barn to milk the cow. He'd likely already brought in the eggs for Belinda because she heard her stirring in the kitchen.

The smell of fresh coffee and warm cinnamon rolls wafted in under the door, filling the room with an aroma that made her stomach growl.

When little Silas had his fill, she lifted him to her shoulder and rubbed his back to make him comfortable and bring a nice burp. By the time she'd finished with him, he was fast asleep again. She laid him back in his cradle and dressed herself in a dark, navy work-dress.

She'd decided, for the sake of being married to Noah, and for her parents, to give up her *Englisch* clothes, which wasn't a problem at all. She'd had enough of that lifestyle, and longed to return to her Amish roots. Certainly now with little Silas, she would not turn from her heritage again. Her intention was to raise her child with the same morals and values she had been brought up with. And when he was old enough to venture out on his own, she would tell him of her experience with the *Englisch* life, and hope that he would not make the same mistakes she had.

Once she'd put her prayer *kapp* in place on her head, she looked at herself in the mirror. She was thankful her mother had brought over her old things from her room at their home. Though she hadn't worn any of it for almost a year, it felt as comfortable as if she'd never stopped wearing it.

She peeked in on her son and kissed his little soft cheek, and then said a quick prayer for him. Leaving the door open so she could listen for him, she went out to the kitchen and Belinda met her with a cup of coffee. She sipped it, enjoying the smoothness. Coffee was not something she was very good at making, and Belinda was showing her how to make it the way she does. She only hoped her coffee would be good enough to make her new husband happy.

They sat at the table, and she offered her a cinnamon roll, and some eggs and bacon. Miranda was starving; she'd not been very hungry the last few days of her pregnancy, but with him nursing, she could not seem to get enough to eat.

"I finished the dress late last night, and I think you'll be pleased."

Miranda smiled. "What about your own dress?"

"My wedding won't be for another few months since I have to take the baptismal classes. Josiah wants to remain in the community, so we will have to get married by the Bishop."

Miranda put a hand on Belinda's. "I'm so happy for you. Since Noah and I didn't break our baptismal vows, we can still see each other. I suppose we will be more like Mennonites."

"As long as we can still be *familye,* none of that matters."

"I was really worried my parents would shun me for what I did," Miranda confessed. "I'm grateful they have been so supportive."

Belinda took a sip of her coffee. "I can't imagine being in your place, and feeling as frightened as you must have been. I'm glad for you that they came around. I was really worried for you."

"I appreciated your prayers, and I'm also grateful you've been supportive of your brother and me."

"All I want is for him to be happy, and I know how much he's always loved you. I'm glad you're going to be my *schweschder.*"

"Me too!"

Belinda picked up the dishes. "Let's say we get you ready. The preacher will be here at noon."

Miranda looked at the battery-operated clock in the kitchen. How had it gotten to be eight o'clock already? She supposed she'd lingered over the baby longer than she'd thought, but time with him seemed to go so fast.

"Do you want me to help with the cooking?"

Belinda pushed her hair back into her *kapp*. "*Jah*, it would be nice to have you here cooking with me, and this is your kitchen now! Besides, I still have packing to do."

Belinda had offered to stay in the *dawdi haus* until November, when she married Josiah, so that she and Noah would have privacy. Since she would be moving in with him and his children once they married, Noah was free to keep the home that belonged to their parents.

A light whimper from the other room made Miranda jump up.

Belinda shooed her. "Go take care of him while I finish up these breakfast dishes. I should be ready to cook once you're finished feeding him."

As she entered the room, she heard Noah come in from the barn. She hoped he would have time to talk to her after she fed the baby, but he began to talk lightly to his sister. She heard laughing and light conversation while she fed Silas.

A light knock startled her.

"It's me," Noah said from the other side of the door. "Is it alright if I come in?"

She put the baby over her shoulder to burp him.

"As long as you don't believe in superstitions!"

He opened the door. "I don't believe in all that bad luck if I see you before the wedding."

He bent down to kiss her and reached for the baby. Putting him over his shoulder, he kissed his head, smelling his hair. "*Bopplin* always smell so *gut!*"

She giggled. "I suppose it's because they're brand new."

He smiled.

"I really came to see you to make sure you hadn't changed your mind about marrying me."

She giggled again. "Are you worried I'm going to leave you at the altar, so-to-speak?"

"A little!"

She stood up and pulled him into her arms and kissed him. "I love you, Noah Byler, and I'm not leaving you ever again."

He grinned. "I just wanted to make certain nothing would get in the way of us getting married today. I've been waiting a long time for this."

"Stop worrying," she said as she kissed him again. "Everything is going to be just fine."

~~~~

Belinda took little Silas from Miranda when her father entered in through the kitchen to take his daughter down the makeshift aisle to marry Noah.

He kissed her cheek and smiled, his eyes becoming misty. "I want you to know that I'm proud of you."

Her lower lip quivered, and tears welled up in her blue eyes. "I was afraid you'd be *shemt.*"

"Nee, I love you, Miranda, and I'm proud of you. I'm going to be the best *grossdaddi* that *boppli* could ever have."

"That means everything to me, *Dat*," she said, wiping her tears.

"Let's go meet Noah; he's been waiting a long time to marry you!"

She nodded, knowing just how long he'd waited, but now, both their dreams were about to come true.

She and her father stepped out of the house and into the yard, walking toward the trellis at the entrance to Belinda's kitchen garden that would now be hers. The preacher stood in front of the white trellis, which had morning glory vines intertwining all the way around it, the blue flowers being the perfect backdrop. Noah stood beside the preacher, smiling and watching her as she walked toward him.

He'd waited so long for this moment, and he was almost anxious to get it over with so they would have it behind them. But he knew how important today was for Miranda, and for that reason, he would try his best to savor the ceremony.

Silas kissed his daughter on the cheek and joined her hand with Noah's, and then sat down beside Elma on one of the shaker chairs they'd brought out from the kitchen.

The sound of clip-clop horse hooves and buggy wheels making their way up the driveway caused the preacher to pause before beginning the ceremony.

"Are you expecting another guest?" he asked.

Noah shook his head. No one except the family members here knew of their wedding, and he couldn't imagine who would be visiting at such an odd hour.

They turned around and watched as Simon drove up the driveway in his family's buggy.

Noah's heart beat hard against his ribs. If Simon was here to make trouble for Miranda and the baby, he would have to fight for her. He wasn't about to let his friend keep him from marrying her.

Chapter Fifteen

"Why is he here now?" Miranda complained.

The last thing they needed was Simon coming here making trouble. She was so close to marrying Noah, and now, Simon was about to ruin everything.

He stepped out of the buggy and walked toward them, dressed in the traditional Amish clothing, complete with a straw hat atop his head. His hair had been cut and his face clean-shaven. It was the cleanest and the most sober that Miranda had seen him in almost a year.

Silas stood up and positioned himself on the other side of his daughter, just in case she needed him to help Noah defend her.

Miranda let out the breath she'd been holding in when he walked past little Silas. When he approached them, his gaze immediately fell to her flattened abdomen.

"I heard you were getting married today; you know how fast news travels in this community. I also heard you had the baby."

"I hope you didn't come here to make trouble for us," Noah said. "I intend to marry Miranda, and there isn't anything you can do to stop it."

"I didn't come here to stop the wedding," he said. "I came here to give you my blessing. I'm sure that means nothing to you, but I just wanted you to know."

He turned to Miranda, his eyes glazing over with tears. "I am sorry for what I did to you. And I know I have no right to know anything about my child, but I pray that you'll let me see the child and be any part of his life."

Miranda squeezed Noah's hand and looked at him, and he nodded as if to say it was okay.

"I had a boy, and I named him Silas—after *mei vadder*. Belinda is holding him—over there." She pointed to Belinda, and the sleeping baby in her arms.

"May I see him?" Simon asked humbly. "I have a son, and I will do everything I can to make him proud of me."

"I'm sorry that you went to jail," Noah started to say.

"I'm not," Simon interrupted him. "It was the best thing that could've happened to me under the circumstances. I had hit rock bottom, and my drinking was out of control. The judge sentenced me to one-year house arrest on my parents' farm."

He chuckled lightly.

"It's funny that I tried so hard to get away from that place, but that was the only place I wanted to be after being in jail." He lifted his pant-leg to show them the monitor that he had clamped to his ankle. "It gives me a one-mile radius so I can work the land, and I knew since our properties were next to each other, I would have enough wiggle room to come over here. That is, if it's alright with the two of you."

Miranda nodded, and Noah extended his hand, shaking it sincerely.

"You're my friend, Simon, and you'll always be welcome in my home. But I'm afraid it's up to Miranda if she wants you to be around the *boppli*."

Simon turned to Miranda, a pleading look on his face. "I'm required to go to meetings twice a week; one for domestic violence prevention so that I never ever hit another human being as long as I live. The other meeting is so that I can stay sober, but I already intended to. I'm a lucky man that my parents agreed to take me back home after all I've done. But I pray that you'll allow me to be a part of my son's life. I'd like to help the two of you raise him."

Miranda sighed. "I forgive you, Simon, but you'll have to prove yourself. And if I see the slightest sign that you're falling back into your old ways, you will not see Silas again until you're sober."

"You've got my word. I know in the past my word meant nothing, but I aim to change that. I'm so sorry for what happened between us, but I pray that you'll give me a chance to do right by you and our child."

"I will—but only one!"

Miranda walked over to Belinda and lifted her infant son from her arms. She kissed his forehead and looked up at Simon, saying a desperate prayer in her head that God would protect her child, even if it meant protecting him from his own father.

"You may see him; you may hold him, but only with me or Noah present."

He shook Noah's hand again and extended his arms toward his child. Miranda slowly transferred the baby to Simon, whose eyes were filled with tears.

"I promise you, wee one," he said, "that I will be the best *dat* to you, and I'll never let you down again. But it seems today, you're going to get another *dat,* and you'll be the luckiest boy in the community, because you will have two *dats*. I intend to make you proud of me."

He looked down at the child, unable to take his eyes off his sweet, innocent face. He'd begun the year wanting to be an *Englischer* more than anything, but now, as he held his Amish baby, he couldn't think of anywhere else he'd rather be than in the community.

Miranda motioned for him to sit beside Belinda with the baby, and then turned to Noah. "Shall we get married now?"

"*Jah,*" he said eagerly. "I've been waiting a long time for this day. Let's get married!"

The End

Please follow me on

Facebook.

Twitter

Pinterest

Instagram

Look for Book Two in this series!

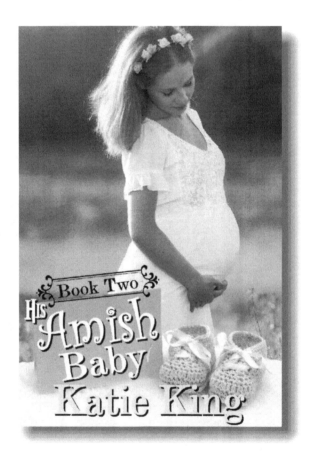